DATE DUE

	DISCARDED		

Demco, Inc. 38-293

Dedicated to Grandma Florence
who loved Rebecca very much

Published in the United States by
Beckham Publications Group, Inc.
P.O. Box 4066, Silver Spring, MD 20914

Library of Congress Control Number:
2006937136

ISBN: 0-931761-37-9

10987654321

When Rebecca was very little,
her favorite plaything
was a stuffed cloth doll
she named Dolly.

She played with Dolly all the time.

Of course Rebecca never went to bed without Dolly by her side.

As Rebecca got older, Dolly started to show its age.

Rebecca's mommy brought her a brand new dolly that was the same as her original dolly, but Rebecca said, "I want MY Dolly!"

Grandma Florence and Grandpa Ed tried
to give her new dollies, but Rebecca said,
"I want MY Dolly!"

Rebecca's daddy brought her a great big
stuffed giraffe. Rebecca liked it, but, she said,
"I want MY Dolly!"

Nana Susan and Grandpa Barry brought her
a beautiful real-looking doll.
Rebecca said, "That's pretty,
but I want MY Dolly!"

Rebecca's mommy tried washing Dolly
since it was getting rather dirty.
Rebecca looked very concerned as she watched.

Dolly was now in very bad shape.
She was all tattered and torn.
Grandpa Ed tried stuffing and sewing her up.

Aunt Rita brought her a stuffed bear and
Uncle Andy brought her a stuffed monkey.
Rebecca said, "They are nice," but she cried,
"I want MY Dolly!"

Aunt Carrie tried giving her a toy dinosaur.

Her other Uncle Andy gave her a stuffed elephant.

Uncle Ira gave her a stuffed toy pig.

Cousin David gave her a stuffed cat.

Cousin Rachel gave her a really pretty blonde doll.

Cousin Alex brought her a toy rabbit.

A family friend, Anita, gave her a stuffed tiger.

Rebecca looked at all the gifts and still she said, "I want MY Dolly!"

When Rebecca took Dolly to the school playground,
all the kids made fun of that dirty, torn and smelly dolly.
They said, "Why don't you throw that old rag thing away?"
Rebecca told them, "I love Dolly, and
I want MY Dolly!"

The teacher told her,
"Rebecca please don't bring that dirty thing
to class anymore." Rebecca said, "I won't bring her…
but I want MY Dolly!"

Now Rebecca's room was filled with lots and lots of new toys and stuffed animals that she thought were really nice. She liked them a lot, but she could not bear to part with her old Dolly.

Rebecca's Daddy had a great idea about how to save Dolly
from just falling apart, and he explained it to Rebecca.
Why not frame Dolly and hang it over her bed,
so it would always be there.

Rebecca finally agreed to the idea, and so she now played with all those new toys that everybody gave her. And she even went to bed with one of the new dollies beside her.